ACCA Paper F7
Financial Reporting

G000292697

First edition 2007, Eleventh edition January 2017

ISBN 9781 5097 0871 0

e ISBN 9781 5097 1009 6

British Library Cataloguing-in-Publication Data
A catalogue record for this book is available from the
British Library

Published by

BPP Learning Media Ltd
BPP House, Aldine Place
142–144 Uxbridge Road
London W12 8AA

www.bpp.com/learningmedia

Printed in the United Kingdom by

Ashford Colour Press Ltd
Unit 600
Fareham Reach, Gosport
Hampshire PO13 0FW

Your learning materials, published by BPP Learning
Media Ltd, are printed on paper obtained from traceable
sustainable sources.

Welcome to BPP Learning Media's ACCA **Passcards** for Paper F7 Financial Reporting.

- They **focus on your exam** and **save you time**.
- They incorporate **diagrams** to kick start your memory.
- They follow the overall **structure** of the BPP Study Texts, but BPP's ACCA **Passcards** are not just a condensed book. Each card has been separately designed for clear presentation. Topics are self contained and can be grasped visually.
- ACCA **Passcards** are still **just the right size** for pockets, briefcases and bags.

Run through the **Passcards** as often as you can during your final revision period. The day before the exam, try to go through the **Passcards** again! You will then be well on your way to passing your exams.

Good luck!

For reference to the Bibliography of the F7 Financial Reporting Passcards please go to:
www.bpp.com/learningmedia/bibliographies

Contents

1: The conceptual framework

The IASB's Framework for the Preparation and Presentation of Financial Statements (1989) has now been replaced by the Conceptual Framework for Financial Reporting (2010).

Conceptual framework – a statement of generally accepted theoretical principles which form the frame of reference for financial reporting.

Advantages	Disadvantages
■ Avoids 'patchwork' or firefighting approach	■ Financial statements are intended for a variety of users – single framework may not suit all
■ Less open to criticism of political/external pressure	■ May need different standards for different purposes
■ Some standards may concentrate on the income statement, others on the balance sheet	■ Preparing and implementing standards is still difficult with a framework

GAAP signifies all the rules, from whatever source, which govern accounting.

Sources for individual countries

- National company law
- National accounting standards
- Local stock exchange requirements
- IASs/IFRSs if applicable

Non-mandatory sources

- Other countries' statutory requirements

In many countries, like the UK, GAAP does not have any statutory or regulatory authority or definition. GAAP is a dynamic concept.

Objectives of financial statements

Financial position

- Statement of financial position

Financial performance

- Statement of profit or loss and other comprehensive income
- Statement of cash flows

Changes in financial performance

- Statement of profit or loss and other comprehensive income
- Statement of cash flows
- Statement of changes in equity
- Notes to the financial statements
- Directors' report

Underlying assumption Going concern

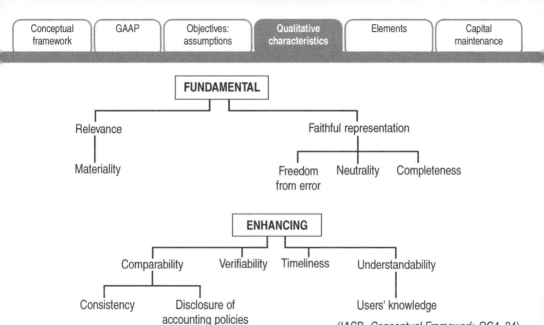

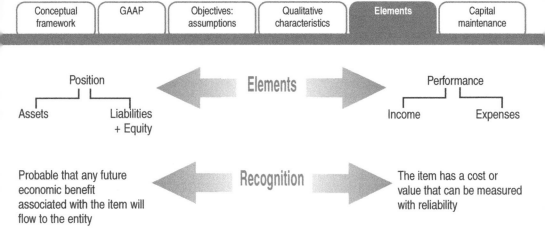

Elements

Position

Assets | Liabilities + Equity

Performance

Income | Expenses

Recognition

Probable that any future economic benefit associated with the item will flow to the entity

The item has a cost or value that can be measured with reliability

Probability = a degree of uncertainty that the future economic benefits will flow to or from the entity.

(IASB, *Conceptual Framework*, 4.27–4.53)

Measurement

Historic cost
(acquisition value)

Current cost (amount if
acquired currently)

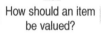

How should an item
be valued?

Present value (present
discounted value of future
net cash inflows item
expected to generate)

Realisable (settlement)
value (amount selling
in current state)

(IASB, *Conceptual Framework*, 4.55)

Financial capital maintenance

Profit is earned if the financial amount of the net assets at the end of a period exceeds the financial amount of net assets at the beginning of a period after excluding any distributions to, and contributions from, owners during period.

Can be measured in either nominal monetary units or units of constant purchasing power.

Physical capital maintenance

Profit is earned if the physical productive capacity (or operating capacity) of the entity at the end of the period exceeds the physical productive capacity at the beginning of the period, after excluding any distributions to and contributions from, owners during the period. This concept requires the current cost basis of measurement.

The selection of the measurement bases and concept of capital maintenance together determine the accounting model used.

(IASB, *Conceptual Framework*, 4.57–4.65)

2: The regulatory framework

Topic List

IASB

IFRS

Criticisms

You'll already have covered the IASB in your earlier studies.

IASB

Financial reporting is governed on a worldwide basis by the International Accounting Standards Board. Decisions on accounting principles are made by the Board and issued in the form of IFRS (IAS).

Remember!

May 2000 – IOSCO gave qualified backing to 30 IAS.

Remember!

EC directive: since 2005 consolidated accounts of listed entities must use IFRS.

The IASB issued 41 IASs. Standards are now called IFRS and 15 IFRSs have been issued so far. The procedure for issuing an IFRS can be summarised as follows.

1. During the early stages of a project, IASB may establish an **Advisory Committee** to give advice on issues arising in the project. Consultation with the Advisory Committee and the Standards Advisory Council occurs throughout the project.

2. IASB may develop and publish **Discussion Documents** for public comment.

3. Following the receipt and review of comments, IASB would develop and publish an **Exposure Draft** for public comment.

4. Following the receipt and review of comments, the IASB would issue a final **International Financial Reporting Standard**.

Criticisms

| **Rigidity** | Criticisms | **Too much choice** |

Rigidity

- Lack of flexibility in applying rules

- Recent standards eg IFRS 9 very detailed and prescriptive

- Rules may not be applicable in all circumstances

Too much choice

- Benchmark treatment and allowed alternatives. These have been largely eliminated.

- Standards may be subject to lobbying or government pressure.

3: Tangible non-current assets

Topic List

IAS 16
IAS 40
IAS 23

IAS 16 should be familiar to you from your earlier studies.

Borrowing costs are covered by IAS 23 (revised).

IAS 16 *Property, plant and equipment* covers all aspects of accounting for these items, which are most tangible non-current assets.

Probable that future economic benefits associated with the assets will flow to the entity ← **Recognition** → Cost of asset can be reliably measured

Initial measurement

Purchase price	Directly attributable costs	Other costs
■ Import duties	■ Site preparation	■ Estimate of dismantling/removal costs and site restoration (IAS 37)
■ Non-refundable purchase taxes	■ Delivery/handling	
■ LESS	■ Testing	■ Finance costs (IAS 23)
■ Trade discounts/rebates	■ Professional fees	

(IAS 16: para. 16)

Subsequent expenditure

Same criteria as initial costs. Otherwise do not capitalise but charge to profit or loss.

Subsequent measurement

Cost model	Revaluation model	Depreciation
■ Cost less accumulated depreciation and accumulated impairment losses	■ Revalued amount (fair value at the date of revaluation) less subsequent accumulated depreciation and impairment losses ■ Revalue sufficiently regularly so carrying amount not materially different from fair value ■ All items of same class should be revalued	■ Systematic basis over useful life reflecting pattern of use of asset's economic benefits ■ Periodic review of useful life and depreciation method and any change accounted for as change in accounting estimate

(IAS 16: paras. 29–31)

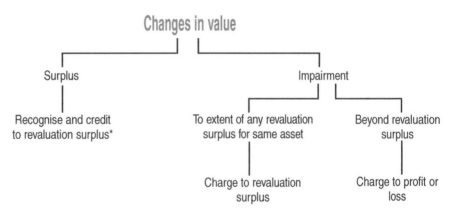

Changes in value

Surplus

Recognise and credit to revaluation surplus*

Impairment

To extent of any revaluation surplus for same asset

Charge to revaluation surplus

Beyond revaluation surplus

Charge to profit or loss

* Unless reversing a previously recognised revaluation decrease of the same asset, in which case recognise as income to the extent of reversal of the previous decrease.

(IAS 16: paras. 36–42)

Investment property is property held to earn rentals or for capital appreciation or both, rather than for:

a) Use in the production or supply of goods or services or for administrative purposes

b) Sale in the ordinary course of business

Owner – occupied property cannot be classified as investment property.

Accounting treatment

An entity can choose to hold investment property under either:

a) The fair value model; or

b) The cost model

This choice will apply to **all** of its investment property.

(IAS 40: paras. 6–8, 30–32)

3: Tangible non-current assets

IAS 23 Borrowing costs

The standard deals with borrowing costs for **self-constructed assets**.

Borrowing costs

Interest and other costs incurred by an entity in connection with the borrowing of funds

Qualifying asset

An asset that necessarily takes a substantial period of time to get ready for its intended sale or use

Included in borrowing costs

- Interest on bank overdrafts and short and long term borrowings
- Amortisation of discounts or premiums related to borrowings
- Amortisation of ancillary costs incurred with the arrangement of borrowings
- Finance charges in respect of leases under IFRS 16
- Exchange differences as far as they are an adjustment to interest costs

Capitalisation is mandatory if the costs are **directly attributable** to the acquisition, construction or production of a qualifying asset.

(IAS 23: paras. 8–12)

4: Intangible assets

Topic List

IAS 38

Goodwill

IAS 38 aims to prescribe the accounting treatment for intangible assets not dealt with under another IFRS. The standard deals with the criteria for recognition and measurement.

Goodwill is a controversial area. It comes up again in connection with group accounts.

Definition

An intangible asset is an identifiable non-monetary asset without physical substance held for use in the production or supply of goods or services, for rental to others, or for administrative purposes.

Recognition

Recognise if and only if:

- It is probable that the future economic benefits that are attributable to the asset will flow to the entity

- The cost of the asset can be measured reliably

Initial measurement

Intangible assets should initially be measured at cost.

(IAS 38: paras. 8–24)

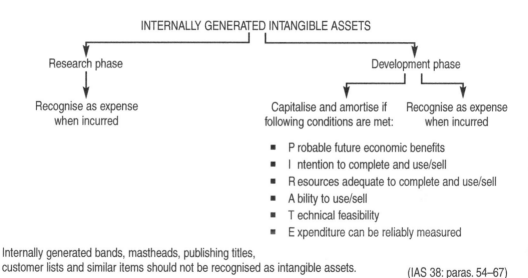

INTERNALLY GENERATED INTANGIBLE ASSETS

Research phase

Recognise as expense
when incurred

Development phase

Capitalise and amortise if
following conditions are met:

Recognise as expense
when incurred

- P robable future economic benefits
- I ntention to complete and use/sell
- R esources adequate to complete and use/sell
- A bility to use/sell
- T echnical feasibility
- E xpenditure can be reliably measured

Internally generated bands, mastheads, publishing titles,
customer lists and similar items should not be recognised as intangible assets.

(IAS 38: paras. 54–67)

Subsequent expenditure

Subsequent expenditure must meet the original recognition criteria to be added to the cost of the intangible asset.

Amortisation

Should be charged on a systematic basis over the useful life of the asset. Should commence when asset available for use. Period and method to be reviewed at each year end.

Intangibles with indefinite useful life are not amortised, but reviewed at least annually for impairment.

Subsequent re-measurement

Cost model: cost less accumulated amortisation and impairment losses

Revaluation model: revalued amount less subsequent accumulated amortisation and impairment losses

Revalued amount is fair value at date of revaluation by reference to an active market

All other assets in the same class should be revalued unless there is no active market for them, in which case the cost model value should be used for those assets.

Revaluations so that the carrying value does not offer materially from fair value

(IAS 38: paras. 97–106)

Impairment losses

The recoverable amount of the asset should be determined at least at each financial year end and any impairment loss should be accounted for in accordance with IAS 36.

Disclosures

Need to make the following disclosures:

- Distinguish between internally generated and other intangible assets

- Useful lives of assets and amortisation methods

- Gross carrying amount and accumulated amortisation at start and end of period

- Where the amortisation is included in the statement of profit or loss and other comprehensive income

- A reconciliation of opening balance to closing balance

- If research and development, how much was charged as expense

(IAS 38: paras. 118–126)

Goodwill can be purchased or be acquired as part of a business combination. In either case, the treatment is capitalisation at cost or fair value under IFRS 3.

Negative goodwill

Arises when acquirer's interest in identifiable net assets exceeds the cost of the combination. Results from **errors** or a **bargain**.

Reassess cost of combination and assets.

Recognise **any remaining** goodwill **immediately** in **profit or loss**.

Goodwill

Future economic benefits arising from assets that are not capable of being individually identified and separately recognised

Recognise as an asset and measure at cost/excess of purchase cost over acquired interest

Do **not amortise**

Test at least annually for **impairment** (IAS 36: para. 90)

You may be asked for a complicated calculation of goodwill as part of a group accounts question.

(IFRS 3: paras. 32–36)

5: Impairment of assets

Topic List

IAS 36

IAS 36 covers impairment of assets.

The aim of IAS 36 *Impairment of assets* is to ensure that assets are carried in the financial statements at no more than their **recoverable amount.** Note that IAS 36 does not apply to non-current assets held for sale which are covered by IFRS 5.

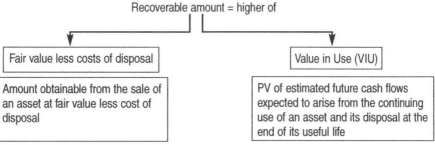

Recoverable amount = higher of

Fair value less costs of disposal

Amount obtainable from the sale of an asset at fair value less cost of disposal

Value in Use (VIU)

PV of estimated future cash flows expected to arise from the continuing use of an asset and its disposal at the end of its useful life

Where it is not possible to estimate the recoverable amount of an individual asset, an entity should determine the recoverable amount of the **cash-generating unit** to which it belongs.

The standard also specifies when an entity should reverse an impairment loss and prescribes certain disclosures for impaired assets.

(IAS 36: paras. 18–23)

Indicators of impairment

A review for impairment of a non-current asset or goodwill should be carried out if events or changes in circumstances indicate that the carrying amount of the non-current asset or goodwill may not be recoverable.

External indicators

- Fall in market value

- Change in technological, legal or economic environment

- Increase in market interest rate likely to affect discount rates

- Carrying amount of entity's net assets > market capitalisation

Internal indicators

- Obsolescence or physical damage

- Adverse changes in use

- Adverse changes in asset's economic performance

It may not be possible to associate cash flows with individual assets so the review of the recoverable amount will often have to be applied to **cash generating units** that contain groups of related assets.

(IAS 36: paras. 7–17)

Calculation of value in use

Include cash flows	Exclude cash flows
■ Directly attributable	■ Any future restructuring to which the enterprise is not yet committed
■ An appropriate proportion that can be allocated on a reasonable and consistent basis	■ Future capital expenditure that will improve/enhance asset in excess of originally assessed standard of performance
■ Net cash flows to be received or paid for the disposal of the asset at the end of its useful life on a fair value basis	■ Financing activities
	■ Income tax receipts or payments

The discount rate should be a pre-tax rate that reflects current market assessments of the time value of money and the risks specific to the asset.

(IAS 36: paras. 30–57)

Allocation of impairment loss

1 To the goodwill allocated to the cash generating unit

2 To all other assets in the cash generating unit on a pro rata basis

Recognition of losses

- Assets carried at historic cost – profit or loss

- Revalued assets – under rules of applicable IAS

- Depreciation adjusted in future periods to allocate the asset's revised carrying amount less residual value over its remaining useful life

(IAS 36: paras. 104–105)

Reversal of past impairments

Where the recoverable amount increases, the resulting reversal should be recognised in the current period to the extent that it increases the carrying amount up to the amount that it would have been (net of amortisation or depreciation) had no impairment loss been recognised in prior years.

- *Individual assets:* Recognise as income immediately unless the asset is carried at revalued amount under another IFRS in which case apply the rules of that IFRS

- *CGUs:* Exact opposite of its original recognition while ensuring that assets are not increased above the lower of their recoverable amount and their carrying amount (after depreciation or amortisation) had there been no impairment loss

- *Goodwill:* Not reversed in subsequent period unless:

  - The impairment was caused by a specific external event of an exceptional nature not expected to recur

  - Subsequent external events have occurred which reverse the effect of that event

(IAS 36: paras. 107–125)

Disclosure

- The amount of impairment losses recognised in the statement of profit or loss and other comprehensive income during the period and the line items affected

- The amount of impairment loss reversals recognised in the statement of profit or loss and other comprehensive income during the period and the line items affected

- The amount of impairment losses debited directly against equity in the period

- The amount of impairment loss reversals credited directly to equity in the period for material impairment losses or loss reversals:

  - The events and circumstances

  - The amount

  - The nature of the asset or cash generating unit

  - For initial losses whether recoverable amount is NSP or VIU (and details of basis of selling price or discount rate as appropriate)

6: Revenue

Topic List

IFRS 15

5-Step model

Performance obligations

IAS 20

IFRS 15 *Revenue from contracts with customers* now replaces IAS 18 *Revenue* and IAS 11 *Construction contracts*.

IFRS 15 *Revenue from contracts with customers*

The core principle of IFRS 15 is that revenue is recognised to depict the transfer of goods or services to a customer.

Transfer of goods and services is based upon transfer of **control** over those goods and services.

A contract with a customer contains a promise to transfer goods or services.

This promise is defined in IFRS 15 as a **performance obligation**.

(IFRS 15: IN7)

The 5-step model in IFRS 15 is:

Step 1: Identify the contract with the customer

Step 2: Identify the separate performance obligations

Step 3: Determine the transaction price

Step 4: Allocate the transaction price to the performance obligations

Step 5: Recognise revenue when (or as) a performance obligation is satisfied

(IFRS 15: IN7)

A performance obligation can be satisfied **at a point in time** or **over time**.

Where a performance obligation is satisfied at a point in time, this will be the point in time at which **control is transferred to the customer**.

Indicators of this are:

- The entity has a right to payment
- The customer has legal title to the asset
- The customer has taken possession of the asset
- Risks and rewards have been transferred
- The customer has accepted the asset

Where a performance obligation is satisfied **over time** it is necessary to establish the amount of performance completed during the accounting period. This can be measured using **output methods** (such as surveys of work completed) or **input methods** (such as labour hours or costs incurred).

Contracts where performance obligations are satisfied over time are common in the construction industry.

(IFRS 15: paras. 31–38)

Contract where performance obligations are satisfied over time

Outcome can be estimated reliably

|

Recognise contract revenue and contract costs by reference to amount of performance obligation satisfied

An entity must determine what amounts to include as revenue and costs in each accounting period

Any expected loss should be recognised as an expense immediately

Outcome cannot be estimated reliably

|

Recognise revenue only to extent of contract costs incurred that it is probable will be recovered. Recognise as expense in period incurred

(IFRS 5: paras. 35–37)

Where the outcome of a contract can be estimated reliably, a proportion of contract revenue and costs should be recognised in profit or loss by reference to the stage of completion (ie a proportion that fairly reflects the amount of work done). This represents the amount of performance obligation satisfied.

The stage of completion can be calculated in various ways including:

Proportion of contract costs incurred:

$$\frac{\text{Costs to date}}{\text{Total estimated costs}} \times \text{Estimated total revenue/costs}$$

Input method

Surveys of work performed:

$$\frac{\text{Work certified}}{\text{Contract price}} \times \text{Estimated total revenue/costs}$$

Output method

(IFRS 5: paras. 39–45)

Disclosure

Statement of profit or loss	
Revenue (x% × total contract revenue)	X
Expenses (x% × total contract cost)	(X)
	X
Expected loss	(X)
Recognised profit/loss	X

Statement of financial position	
Contract asset/liability	
Contract costs incurred	X
Recognised profits less recognised losses	X
	X
Less amounts invoiced to date	(X)
	X/(X)
Trade receivables	
Amounts invoiced to date	X
Less cash received	(X)
	X

IAS 20 *Accounting for government grants and disclosure of government assistance* requires the following accounting treatment.

Grants related to income

Either show as credit in profit or loss (other income) or deduct in reporting the related expense

Grants related to assets

Treat as deferred income and credit to profit or loss on systematic rational basis over useful life of asset OR deduct grant in arriving at carrying value of asset and recognise as income over asset's life by means of reduced depreciation charge

Disclose:

- Accounting policy

- Nature and extent of grants recognised

- Unfulfilled conditions and other contingencies relating to grants recognised

Recognise only when reasonable assurance that any conditions will be met and monies received.

(IAS 20: paras. 24–31)

7: Introduction to groups

Topic List

Group accounts

IFRS 10

Consolidation is a very important area of your Paper F7 syllabus, likely to appear as a long question in Part C.

This chapter looks at the basic definitions and relevant accounting standards.

Subsidiary

An entity that is controlled by another entity known as the parent

Associate

An entity in which an investor has significant influence and which is neither a subsidiary nor a joint venture of the investor

Control: An investor controls an investee when the investor is exposed, or has rights to, variable returns from its involvement with the investee and has the ability to affect those returns through power over the investee

Significant influence: The power to participate in the financial and operating policy decisions of an economic activity but not control or joint control over those policies

Easy marks can be gained for reproducing these definitions. But make sure you understand them!

(IFRS 10: App A)

Summary of classification and treatment

Investment	Criteria	Required treatment in group accounts
Subsidiary	Control (>50% rule)	Full consolidation (see Chapter 9)
Associate	Significant influence (20% + rule)	Equity accounting (see Chapter 11)
Investment which is none of the above	Assets held for accretion of wealth	As for single entity accounts

Other provisions of IFRS 10

Consolidated financial statements:

The financial statements of a group presented as those of a single economic entity

Exemption

- A parent need not prepare group accounts if it is itself a wholly owned subsidiary
- If it is partially owned and the other owners do not object
- Its securities are not publicly traded
- The ultimate or intermediate parent publishes IFRS – compliant consolidated accounts
- Disclosures apply

Exclusion

IAS 27 effectively removed any exclusions. Subsidiaries held for sale must be accounted for in accordance with IFRS 5.

Other

- Different reporting dates – adjustments should be made
- Uniform accounting policies – if not, disclose why. Adjustments should be made on consolidation

(IFRS 10: para. 4)

8: The consolidated statement of financial position

Topic List

This chapter introduces the basic techniques you will need to prepare a consolidated statement of financial position.

IFRS 3 brings another issue into consolidation questions. It has an option to value the non-controlling interest at fair value. Look out for this.

Purpose	To show the assets and liabilities which it controls and their ownership
Assets and liabilities	Always 100% P plus S providing P has control
Share capital	P only
Reason	Simply reporting to the parent's shareholders in another form
Retained earnings	100% P plus group share of post-acquisition retained reserves of S less consolidation adjustments
Reason	To show the extent to which the group actually owns assets and liabilities included in the statement of financial position
Non-controlling interest	NCI share of S's consolidated assets less liabilities **or** fair value*
Reason	To show the extent to which other parties own assets and liabilities but under the control of the parent

* **Note.** If the NCI is at fair value you may be given a) the share price or b) the fair value of the NCI

IFRS 3

IFRS 3 gives entities the option to value the non-controlling interest at **fair value**. This affects the goodwill and non-controlling interest calculations. The options are as follows: [P holds 60% of S. Goodwill impaired by $100,000. Fair value of NCI $900,000]

<table>
<tr><th colspan="2">Non-controlling interest at share of net assets</th><th colspan="2">Non-controlling interest at fair value</th></tr>
<tr><td>Goodwill</td><td>$'000</td><td><strong>Goodwill</strong></td><td>$'000</td></tr>
<tr><td>Consideration transferred</td><td>1,600</td><td>Consideration transferred</td><td>1,600</td></tr>
<tr><td>Non-controlling interest (2,000 × 40%)</td><td>800</td><td>Non-controlling interest</td><td>900</td></tr>
<tr><td>Net assets</td><td>(2,000)</td><td>Net assets</td><td>(2,000)</td></tr>
<tr><td>Goodwill</td><td>400</td><td>Goodwill</td><td>500</td></tr>
<tr><td>Impairment</td><td>(100)</td><td>Impairment</td><td>(100)</td></tr>
<tr><td>Carrying value</td><td>300</td><td>Carrying value</td><td>400</td></tr>
</table>

Note that the total goodwill is now $400,000, reflecting the $100,000 goodwill attributable to the non-controlling interest.

8: The consolidated statement of financial position

Non-controlling interest at end of reporting period

The option to value the non-controlling interest at fair value applies to non-controlling interest **at acquisiton**. However, it will affect the valuation of non-controlling interest **at the year end**.

Under the two options above, this will be as follows (net assets now $3m)

Non-controlling interest at share of net assets		**Non-controlling interest at fair value**	
	$'000		$'000
S net assets	3,000	Fair value of NCI	900
NCI 40%	1,200	NCI share of increase in net assets	
		$((3,000 - 2,000) \times 40\%)$	400
		Goodwill impairment $(100 \times 40\%)$	(40)
			1,260

Fair value options

If you are required to account for NCI at fair value there are two options:

1) You may be told what fair value of the NCI is

2) You may be given the share price at the date of acquisition

The examination team has said that they will usually examine NCI at FV, so be prepared for this.

1 Read the question and the requirements.

2 Group structure noting dates of acquisition.

3 Prepare necessary proforma required by question.
- Level of detail is dictated by level of detail in question
- Leave out cost of investment
- Include line for non-controlling interest

4 Consider adjustments and note on question paper.
- Dividends
- PUP
- Revaluation to fair value
- Reconciliation of intra-group balances
- Support adjustments by working eg PUP

5 Aggregate adjusted assets and liabilities.
- Incorporate adjustments
- Cancel any intra-group items eg current a/c balances, dividends, loan notes

6 Share capital of P only.

7 Goodwill

Consideration transferred		X
Non-controlling interest		X
Net assets acquired as represented by		
Share capital	X	
Share premium	X	
Reserves	X	
Retained earnings	X	
		(X)
Goodwill (gain on bargain purchase)		X/(X)

> Remember that goodwill is retained in the statement, subject to impairment reviews. Remember rules for gain on a bargain purchase.

Retained earnings

	P	S
8 Per question	X	X
Adjustments as noted on question paper	X/(X)	X/(X)
	X	Y
Share of S post acquisition %	X	
	X	
Any impairment of goodwill	(X)	
	X	

9 Non-controlling interest

Fair value at acquisition	X
Share of post-acquisition retained earnings (per 8)	X
Share of any goodwill impairment	(X)
	X

Fair values (IFRS 3)

On consolidation, the fair value of the consideration paid for a subsidiary is compared with the fair value of the net assets.

IFRS 3 sets out rules determining the fair value of the purchase consideration, the fair value of identifiable assets and liabilities acquired and the fair value of specific net assets.

Fair value (IFRS 3)

The amount for which an asset could be exchanged, or a liability settled, between knowledgeable, willing parties in an arm's length transaction.

New definition (IFRS 13)

The price that would be received to sell an asset or paid to transfer a liability in an orderly transaction between market participants at the measurement date.

(IFRS 13: App A)

Fair value adjustment calculations

Goodwill is the difference between the cost of the acquisition and the acquirer's interest in the fair value of the identifiable assets and liabilities. So far we have used book value for the assets and liabilities. However, IFRS 3 states that we should use fair value (IFRS 3: para. 18). Therefore revaluations may be necessary to ensure that book value is equal to fair value.

Subsidiary		Parent
Revalues assets and liabilities to fair value	**OR**	Revalues assets and liabilities as a consolidation adjustment
		Subsidiary's books unchanged

In the exam the usual scenario is that the subsidiary has not revalued to fair value and so a consolidation adjustment is needed.

9: The consolidated statement of profit or loss and other comprehensive income

Topic List

Consolidated statement of profit or loss

Consolidated statement of profit or loss and other comprehensive income

Disposals

Under the revised IAS 1 the full statement is now called the 'statement of profit or loss and other comprehensive income'. At F7 level some questions will only require the first part of the statement, which will be referred to as the 'statement of profit or loss.' (IAS 1: para. 10)

Purpose	To show the results of the group for an accounting period as if it were a single entity
Sales revenue to profit after tax	100% P + 100% S (excluding dividend receivable from subsidiary and adjustments for intra-group transactions)
Reason	To show the results of the group which were controlled by the parent
Intra-group sales	Strip out intra-group activity from both sales revenue and cost of sales
Unrealised profit on intra-group sales	(a) Goods sold by P: increase cost of sales by unrealised profit
	(b) Goods sold by S: increase cost of sales by full amount of unrealised profit and decrease non-controlling interest by their share of unrealised profit
Depreciation	If the value of S's non-current assets have been subjected to a fair value uplift then any additional depreciation must be charged in the consolidated statement of profit or loss. The non-controlling interest will need to be adjusted for their share.

Transfer of non-current assets	Expenses must be increased by any profit on the transfer and reduced by any additional depreciation arising from the increased carrying value of the asset.
	The unrealised profit is deducted from the profit of the entity making the sale. The excess depreciation is credited back to the entity holding the asset.
	For instance, P transfers an asset with a carrying value of $1,000 to S for $1,100. Depreciation is 10% p.a. $100 is debited to P's statement of profit or loss and $10 is credited to the transferee. The carrying amount of the asset is reduced by $90.
Non-controlling interests	NCI% of S's PAT

Consolidated statement of profit or loss

Adjustments required

- Eliminate **intra group sales and purchases**
- Eliminate **unrealised profit** on intra group purchases still in inventory at the year end
- Eliminate **intra group dividends**
- Split profit for the year between group and NCI

Procedure

- **Combine all P and S results** from revenue to profit after tax. Time apportion where the acquisition is mid-year.
- Exclude **intra group investment** income
- **Calculate NCI** (NCI% × PAT)

Unrealised profits and losses:

Only where S sells to P, allocate the unrealised profit between NCI and P: *Debit* group retained earnings, *Debit* NCI, *Credit* inventory

Consolidated statement of comprehensive income

If there is a revaluation gain or loss in the parent or subsidiary you will prepare a consolidated statement of profit or loss and other comprehensive income. This will only require a few additions to the consolidated statement of profit or loss.

Revaluation gain in parent		Revaluation gain in subsidiary (80%)	
	$'000		$'000
Profit for the year	8,000*	Profit for the year	8,000*
Other comprehensive income:		Other comprehensive income:	
Gains on property revaluation	2,000	Gains on property revaluation	2,000
Total comprehensive income for the year	10,000	Total comprehensive income for the year	10,000
Total comprehensive income attributable to:		Total comprehensive income attributable to:	
Owners of the parent (5,000 + 2,000)	7,000	Owners of the parent (5,000 + (2,000 × 80%)	6,600
Non-controlling interest	3,000	Non-controlling interest (3,000 + (2,000 × 20%))	3,400
	10,000		10,000

*3,000 attributable to NCI

Disposals

When a subsidiary is disposed of in full, the profit on disposal is calculated as follows:

	$	$
Proceeds of disposal		X
Carrying amount at date of disposal:		
Net assets	X	
Goodwill	X	
Less NCI	(X)	
		(X)
Profit on disposal		X

Note that where NCI is measured at fair value the amount attributable to NCI will include the NCI % of goodwill at disposal date.

10: Accounting for associates

Topic List

Associates

As you know, an investment can be carried at cost, fully consolidated or accounted for using the equity method, depending on the degree of control exercised. An associate is accounted for using the equity method.

Individual investor's books

- Carry at cost, or
- In accordance with IFRS 9 as an equity investment

Statement of financial position

Initial cost	X
Add/less: post acquisition share of profits/losses (before dividends)	X/(X)
Less: post-acquisition dividends received to avoid double counting	(X)
Carrying value	X

Consolidated financial statements

Use equity method unless:

- Investment acquired and held exclusively with a view to disposal soon
- Investor ceases to have significant influence

In these cases record at cost.

Statement of profit or loss

Group share of associate's PAT

11: Financial instruments

Topic List

IAS 32

IFRS 9

IFRS 7

A financial instrument is defined in IAS 32 as '(IAS 32: para. 11) any contract that gives rise to both a financial asset of one entity and a financial liability or equity instrument of another'. IAS 39 deals with how financial investments are measured and IFRS 7 covers disclosure.

IFRS 9 is the most recent standard which deals with classification and measurement of assests. It now replaces IAS 39 for all issues covered by the F7 syllabus.

Because of the inherent difficulties in this complex area, it is hard for users to assess the nature, amount and cost of an entity's debt and equity resources.

Before IAS 32 and IAS 39 many financial instruments were treated as off balance sheet finance and invisible to the user of accounts. Because of their significance, the IASB tackled the project in 3 phases:

1. IAS 32: *Presentation* (1995) ensured the user was aware of the instruments and risks

2. IAS 39: *Recognition and Measurement* (1998) prescribed specific accounting treatment as an interim measure

Both standards were revised in December 2003 and IAS 39 is now being replaced by IFRS 9.

3. IFRS 7: *Disclosure* (2005) effective from 1 January 2007 specifies disclosures required for financial instruments

Financial instrument:

Any contract that gives rise to a financial asset of one entity and a financial liability or equity instrument of another

Financial asset:

Cash; equity instrument of another entity; contractual right to receive cash/other financial assets; contract that can be settled in the entity's own equity instruments and may be either a derivative or a non-derivative

(IAS 32: para. 11)

IAS 32 presentation

- Financial instruments should be classified as either:
  - Liability (debt) or
  - Equity
- Compound instruments (exhibiting characteristics of both) must be split into their debt and equity components
- Substance rather than legal form applies (eg redeemable preference shares are a financial liability)
- Interest, dividends, loss or gains relating to a financial instrument claimed as a liability are reported in the I/S, while distributions to holders of equity instruments are debited directly to equity (in the SOCIE)
- Offset of a financial asset and liability is only allowed where there is a legally enforceable right and the entity intends to settle net or simultaneously

Financial liability:

Contractual obligation to deliver cash/other financial asset; contractual obligation to exchange financial instruments under potentially unfavourable conditions

Equity instrument:

Contract that evidences a residual interest in the assets of an entity after deducting all its liabilities

(IAS 32: para. 11)

IFRS 9

IFRS 9 deals with recognition and measurement of financial assets and liabilities. It classifies assets on the basis of the entity's **business model** and the cash flow characteristic of the financial asset.

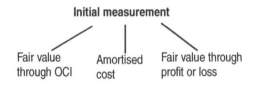

Initial measurement

Fair value through OCI   Amortised cost   Fair value through profit or loss

(IFRS 9: paras. 4.1–4.2)

Subsequent measurement: financial assets (FA)

Amortised cost

- Where held to collect contractual cash flows as specified dates

Fair value

- Financial assets at fair value through profit or loss
- Equity investments
- Assets held for trading **and** to collect contracted cash flows are measured at fair value through OCI

Subsequent measurement: financial liabilities (FL)

Fair value

- Financial liabilities at fair value through profit or loss
- Has to be held for trading and classified at inception at FV through profit or loss
- Gain or loss as a result of change in **credit risk** must go through **OCI**

Amortised cost

- All others

(IFRS 9: paras. 5.1–5.4)

Calculations

The method used in the following example applies to deep discount bonds and other similar instruments (including zero coupon bonds).

Debt issued for $400,000 (nominal) on 1.1.20X1 for proceeds of $315,526; redeemed for $400,000 (ie par) on 31.12.20X5

Interest rate = 4%

Effective interest rate = 9.5%

	$
Annual interest payments (4% × $400,000 × 5)	80,000
Deep discount $(400,000 – 315,526)	84,474
	164,474

At inception	DEBIT	Cash	$315,526
	CREDIT	Liability	$315,526

Year	P or L charge *$	Actual interest payable $	Rolled up interest charged to P or L $	Closing liability $
20X1	29,975	16,000	13,975	329,501
20X2	31,303	16,000	15,303	344,804
20X3	32,756	16,000	16,756	361,560
20X4	34,348	16,000	18,348	379,908
20X5	36,092	16,000	20,092	400,000
	164,474	80,000	84,474	

*9.5% × opening liability in statement of financial position (315,526).

Fair value is measured as quoted market price in an active market where possible.

11: Financial instruments

Gains and losses (on remeasurement to fair value)

- Held at fair value: profit or loss

- Investments in equity instruments: reported in equity and under other comprehensive income

Impairment

- Impairment review where evidence of financial asset being impaired

- Original effective interest rate should be used when discounting future cash flows to calculate the impairment

- Impairment loss is charged to profit or loss

- Where investment in equity instrument suffers impairment loss, this is recognised in statement of changes in equity and under other comprehensive income

(IFRS 9: para. 5.5)

IFRS 7: *Financial instruments: Disclosure*

The objective of IFRS 7 is to require entities to provide disclosures in their financial statements that enable users to evaluate:

(a) The significance of financial instruments for the entity's financial position and performance

(b) The nature and extent of risks arising from financial instruments to which the entity is exposed and how the entity manages those risks

This information can influence a user's assessment of the financial position and performance of an entity and of the nature of its future cash flows.

In addition to the numerical disclosures required by IFRS 9, IFRS 7 encourages a **narrative commentary** by issuers of financial instruments, which will enable users to understand their attitude to risk.

(IFRS 7: paras. 1,7)

You will not be examined on the risks inherent in financial instruments.

12: Leasing

Topic List

Leases

Accounting treatment

Disclosures: lessees

Leasing transactions are very common in practice. It is important that you get to grips with the basics of IFRS 16.

IFRS 16 *Leasing*

IFRS 16 defines a lease as follows:

'A contract, or part of a contract, that conveys the right to use an asset (the underlying asset) for a period of time in exchange for consideration'. (IFRS 16: Appendix A)

Accounting treatment

Lease	Short-term or low-value lease
■ Recognise right-of-use asset (measured at present value of lease payments plus lease payments before start date plus indirect costs plus dismantling costs less incentives received)	■ Charge rentals on a straight line basis or other systematic basis over lease period
■ Set up lease liability	■ Statement of financial position
■ Repayments split between finance charge and capital	– Only accruals/prepayments for rentals
■ Statement of financial position	■ Statement of profit or loss
– Carrying amount of right-of-use asset	– Rental expense
– Lease liability	
■ Statement of profit or loss	
– Depreciation	
– Finance charge	

Statement of financial position

1 **Non current assets**

Included in the carrying amount of plant and equipment is $X in respect of right-of-use assets

2 **Non current liabilities**

Lease liabilities (note 4) X

3 **Current liabilities**

Lease liabilities (note 4) X

Accruals (note 4) X

4 **Lease liabilities: reconciliation of minimum lease payments and present value**

Within one year	X (gross)
Later than one year and not later than five years	X (gross)
Later than five years	X (gross)
Less future finance charges	(X)
Present value of lease liabilities	X

5 **Present value of lease liabilities**

Within one year	X (net)
Later than one year and not later than five years	X (net)
Later than five years	X (net)
	X

Note. The lease payments include the finance charge element. The present value is the capital element only of the lease liability.

6 **Short-term or low-value leases**

The future minimum lease payments under short-term or low value leases are as follows:

Within one year	X
Later than one year and not later than five years	X
Later than five years	X
	X

Statement of profit or loss and other comprehensive income

Although not specifically required by IFRS 16, companies tend to also disclose the following in the notes.

 7 **Profit from operations**

Profit from operations is stated after charging:

Depreciation on right-of-use assets   X

 8 **Finance cost**

Finance charge on leases: X

13: Provisions and events after the reporting period

Topic List

IAS 37

IAS 10

IAS 37 and IAS 10 should both be familiar to you from your earlier studies. IAS 37 is particularly topical in the light of increasing environmental awareness.

IAS 37

IAS 37 *Provisions, contingent liabilities and contingent assets* was brought in to remedy some abuses of provisions.

- Entities should **not provide** for **costs** that need to be incurred to **operate in the future,** if those **costs could be avoided** by the entity's future actions

- **Costs of restructuring** are to be recognised as a provision only when the entity has an **obligation** to carry out the restructuring

- The **full amount** of any **decommissioning costs** or environmental liabilities should be **recognised from the date on which they arise**

Provision

A liability of uncertain timing or amount. Liabilities are obligations to transfer economic benefits as a result of past transactions or events.

Contingent liability

Should be disclosed unless the possibility of any outflow of economic benefits to settle it is remote

Contingent asset

Should be disclosed where an inflow of economic benefits is probable

(IAS 37: para. 10)

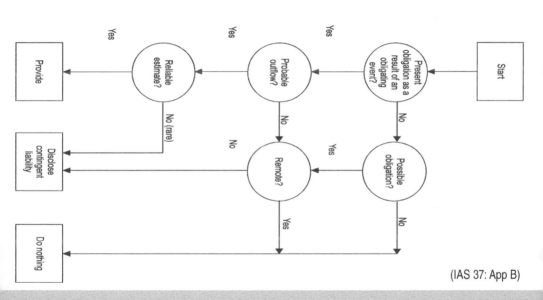

(IAS 37: App B)

13: Provisions and events after the reporting period

IAS 10 *Events after the reporting period* distinguishes between **adjusting** and **non-adjusting** events.

Adjusting events provide evidence of conditions that existed at the end of the reporting period and require adjustment to be made to the financial statements.

(IAS 10: para. 3)

14: Inventories and biological assets

Topic List

IAS 2

IAS 41

You've met inventory and inventory valuation in your earlier studies, so only a brief summary is given here.

Biological assets are regulated by IAS 41 Agriculture

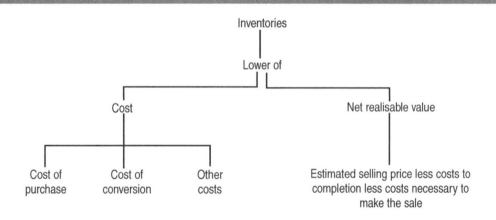

Permitted treatment of cost: FIFO or weighted average

LIFO is not permitted under IAS 2 *Inventories*.

(IAS 2: para. 9)

IAS 41: *Agriculture*

IAS 41 identifies the **critical events** associated with biological transformation as growth, procreation, production and degeneration.

In the statement of financial position biological assets should be measured at **fair value** less estimated point-of-sale costs. Agricultural produce derived from biological assets is also measured at fair value less estimated point-of-sale costs.

(IAS 41: para. 7)

15: Taxation

Topic List

Current tax

Deferred tax

Taxable temporary differences

Deductible temporary differences

Disclosure

In nearly all countries entities pay tax on their trading income. There are two aspects to this: current tax and deferred tax.

Most students find deferred tax more difficult than current tax, so study this section carefully. Questions in Paper F7 should not generally be too complicated.

IAS 12

IAS 12 covers both current and deferred tax. Current tax is fairly easy.

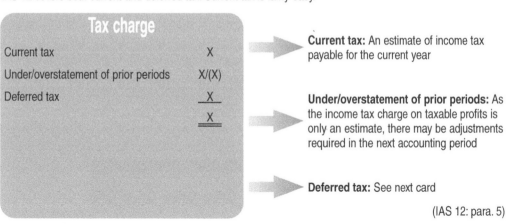

Tax charge	
Current tax	X
Under/overstatement of prior periods	X/(X)
Deferred tax	X
	X

Current tax: An estimate of income tax payable for the current year

Under/overstatement of prior periods: As the income tax charge on taxable profits is only an estimate, there may be adjustments required in the next accounting period

Deferred tax: See next card

(IAS 12: para. 5)

The tax charge in the income statement often bears little relationship to the profit before tax figure because of the differences which exist between tax rules and financial accounting principles.

Accounting for deferred tax

Is recognition of the item different ————— No ————→ No deferred tax implications
for tax and accounts purposes?

    Yes

Is the difference potentially ————— No ————→ No deferred tax implications
only temporary in nature?   (permanent difference)

                                  Liability method

    Yes

Recognise a deferred tax asset or liability using the rate of income tax enacted by end of reporting period that is expected to apply to the period when the asset is realised or the liability settled.

(IAS 12: paras. 7–16)

1 Timing differences

Temporary timing differences arise as a result of the fact that certain items of income/expenditure are dealt with for tax purposes on a receipts basis and on an accruals basis for accounts purposes.

At the end of the reporting period, the timing difference is equivalent to the difference between the accrued income asset and the tax base of the income (amount received ie nil).

2 Specific timing differences – accelerated capital allowances

When tax (or 'capital') allowances/tax depreciation rates are available at a rate higher than the accounting depreciation rates applied to the same assets.

On a cumulative basis calculated as:

Net book value (NBV)	X
Less tax written down value (TWDV)	(X)
	X

3 Revaluations

The revaluation of an asset will create a temporary difference when it is incorporated in the statement of financial position, insofar as the profit or loss that would result from realisation at the revalued amount is taxable. Deferred tax is normally provided out of the revaluation surplus.

(IAS 12: para. 16)

Deductible temporary differences

Deductible temporary differences arise since certain items of expenditure are dealt with for tax purposes on a payments basis and on an accruals basis for accounts purposes.

At the end of the reporting period, the timing difference is equivalent to differences between the accrual and the tax base of the payment (amount paid ie nil).

(IAS 12: para. 24)

Disclosure

Statement of financial position

Deferred tax liability

Balance brought forward	X
Amount charged/(credited) to profit or loss	X/(X)
Amount charged/(credited) to equity	X/(X)
Balance carried forward	X

Statement of profit or loss and other comprehensive income

Current tax	X
Under/overstatement of prior periods	X/(X)
Deferred tax	X
	X

16: Presentation of published financial statements

Topic List

Statement of financial position

Statement of profit or loss and other comprehensive income

Changes in equity

Other matters

All of your studies for Paper F7 will be concerned with the accounts of limited liability companies, so it is important that you are familiar with the IAS 1 formats.

Statement of financial position | Statement of profit or loss and other comprehensive income | Changes in equity | Other matters

Statement of financial position (IAS 1 revised)	20X7 $'000	20X7 $'000	20X6 $'000	20X6 $'000
Assets				
Non-current assets				
Property, plant & equipment	X		X	
Goodwill	X		X	
Other intangible assets	X		X	
Investments in associates	X		X	
Available-for-sale investments	X		X	
		X		X
Current assets				
Inventories	X		X	
Trade receivables	X		X	
Other current assets	X		X	
Cash and cash equivalents	X		X	
		X		X
Total assets		X		X
Equity and liabilities				
Equity attributable to owners of the parent				
Share capital	X		X	
Other reserves	X		X	
Retained earnings	X		X	
		X		X
Non-controlling interest		X		X
Total equity		X		X
Non current liabilities				
Long-term borrowings	X		X	
Deferred tax	X		X	
Long-term provisions	X		X	
Total non-current liabilities		X		X
Current liabilities				
Trade and other payables	X		X	
Short term borrowings	X		X	
Current portion of long-term borrowings	X		X	
Current tax payable	X		X	
Short-term provisions	X		X	
Total current liabilities		X		X
Total equity and liabilities		X		X

(IAS 1: para. 1G)

Statement of profit or loss and other comprehensive income (IAS 1 revised)

	20X2 $'000	20X1 $'000
Revenue	X	X
Cost of sales	(X)	(X)
Gross profit	X	X
Other income	X	X
Distribution costs	(X)	(X)
Administrative expenses	(X)	(X)
Other expenses	(X)	(X)
Finance costs	(X)	(X)
Share of profit of associates	X	X
Profit before tax	X	X
Income tax expense	(X)	(X)
Profit for the year	X	X
Other comprehensive income:		
Items that will not be reclassified to profit or loss:		
Investments in equity instruments	X	X
Gains on property revaluation	X	X
Income tax relating to components of other comprehensive income	(X)	(X)
Other comprehensive income for the year, net of tax	X	X
Total comprehensive income for the year	X	X
Profit attributable to:		
Owners of the parent	X	X
Non-controlling interest	X	X
	X	X
Total comprehensive income for the year	X	X
Total comprehensive income attributable to:		
Owners of the parent	X	X
Non-controlling interest	X	X
	X	X

Statement of changes in equity (IAS 1 revised)

	Share capital $'000	Retained earnings $'000	Revaluation surplus $'000	Total $'000	Non-controlling interest $'000	Total equity $'000
Balance at 1 January 20X6	X	X	X	X	X	X
Changes in accounting policy		X		X	X	X
Restated balance	X	X	X	X	X	X
Changes in equity for 20X6:						
Dividends		(X)		(X)		(X)
Total comprehensive income for the year		X	X	X	X	X
Balance at 31 December 20X6	X	X	X	X	X	X
Changes in equity for 2007:						
Issue of share capital	X			X		X
Dividends		(X)		(X)		(X)
Total comprehensive income for the year		X	X	X	X	X
Transfer to retained earnings		X	(X)			
Balance at 31 December 20X7	X	X	X	X	X	X

IAS 1

The standard suggests that all sets of financial statements should apply the disclosures. An entity must explain all departures and, if relevant, why by following IAS/IFRS fair presentation is not achieved.

Current assets

- Expected to be realised/held for sale in normal course of entity's operating cycle

- Held for trading purposes and expected to be realised within 12 months

- Cash or cash equivalent asset not restricted in use

All other assets are non-current. Each entity must decide whether to present current/non-current assets/liabilities separately. If not, present them in order of liquidity.

(IAS 1: para. 66)

17: Reporting financial performance

Topic List

IAS 8

IFRS 5

Foreign currency

This chapter is largely concerned with the statement of profit or loss. There is no one single IFRS concerned with reporting financial performance as there is in the UK.

IAS 8 *Accounting Policies, Changes in Accounting Estimates and Errors*

Should include all items of income and expense for the period (ie not hidden in reserves) unless an IAS requires/permits otherwise.

Accounting policies

Accounting policies are the specific principles, bases, conventions, rules and practices applied by an entity in preparing and presenting statements.

An entity follows extant Standards and Interpretations when determining its accounting policies.

In the absence of a Standard or Interpretation covering a specific transaction, other event or condition, management uses its judgement to develop an accounting policy which results in information that is relevant and reliable, considering in the following order:

1 Standards or Interpretations dealing with similar and related issues

2 The *Conceptual Framework* definitions and recognition criteria

3 Other national GAAPs based on a similar conceptual framework (providing the treatment does not conflict with extant Standards, Interpretations or the *Conceptual Framework*)

(IAS 8: paras. 7–12)

Changes in accounting policy

Only allowed if:

- Required by standard or interpretation
- The change will provide more relevant or reliable information about events or transactions

Accounting treatment:

- Restate prior year statement of profit or loss and other comprehensive income and statement of financial position

- Restate opening balance of retained earnings

- Include as second line of SOCIE

- Show effect on prior period at foot of prior year SOCIE

(IAS 8: paras. 14)

Changes in accounting estimates

Apply **prospectively**, ie in the current period (and future periods if also affected)

Prior period errors

Omissions from and misstatements in the entity's financial statements for one or more periods

Correct material prior period errors retrospectively in the first set of financial statements authorised for issue after their discovery.

- Restate comparative amounts for each prior period presented in which the error occurred
- Restate the opening balances of assets, liabilities and equity for the earliest prior period presented
- Include any adjustment to opening equity as the second line of the statement of changes in equity
- Disclose the nature of the error and the amount of the correction to prior periods for each line item in each period affected

Where it is impracticable to determine the period-specific effects or the cumulative effect of the error, the entity corrects the error from the earliest period/date practicable (and discloses that fact).

(IAS 8: paras. 32–42)

IFRS 5 *Non-current assets held for sale and discontinued operations* was published in 2004.

Definitions

Discontinued operation	A component of an entity that either has been disposed of or is classified as held for sale and:
	(a) Represents a separate major line of business or geographical area of operations
	(b) Is part of a single co-ordinated plan to dispose of a separate major line of business or geographical area of operations, or
	(c) Is a subsidiary acquired exclusively with a view to resale
Component of an entity	Operations and cash flows that can be clearly distinguished, operationally and for financial reporting purposes, from the rest of the entity
Disposal group	A group of assets to be disposed of (by sale or otherwise) together as a group in a single transaction; **and** liabilities directly associated with those assets that will be transferred in the transaction
Asset held for sale	Its carrying amount will be recovered principally through sale rather than continuing use

(IFRS 5: App A)

Non-current assets held for sale

Criteria

- The asset (or disposal group) must be available for immediate sale in its present condition, subject only to usual and customary sales terms and

- The sale must be highly probable.

  For this to be the case:

  - The appropriate level of **management** must be **committed** to a plan to sell

  - An **active programme** to **locate a buyer** and complete the plan must have been initiated

  - The asset (or disposal group) must be **actively marketed** for sale at a price that is reasonable in relation to its current fair value

  - The sale should be expected to qualify for recognition as a completed sale **within one year** from the date of classification as held for sale (subject to limited specified exceptions)

  - Actions required to complete the plan should indicate that it is **unlikely** that **significant** changes to the plan will be made or that the plan will be withdrawn

Presentation

Assets and disposal groups (including associated liabilities) classified as held for sale are presented:

- On the face of the statement of financial position

- Separately from other assets and liabilities

- Normally as **current** assets and liabilities (not offset)

Measurement

An entity must measure a non-current asset or disposal group classified as held for sale at the **lower of**:

- Carrying amount

- Fair value less costs to sell.

Immediately before initial classifications, measure asset per applicable IFRS. Any impairment loss accounted for as normal.

Non-current assets/disposal groups classified as held for sale are **not depreciated**.

(IFRS 5: paras. 6–12)

Proforma disclosure

XYZ GROUP – STATEMENT OF PROFIT OR LOSS
FOR THE YEAR ENDED 31 DECEMBER 20X7

	20X7 $'000	20X6 $'000
Continuing operations		
Revenue	X	X
Cost of sales	(X)	(X)
Gross profit	X	X
Other income	X	X
Distribution costs	(X)	(X)
Administrative expenses	(X)	(x)
Other expenses	(X)	(X)
Finance costs	(X)	(X)
Share of profit of associates	X	X
Profit before tax	X	X
Income tax expense	(X)	(X)
Profit for the year from continuing operations	X	X
Discontinued operations		
Profit for the year from discontinued operations	X	X
Profit for the year	X	X
Profit attributable to		
Owners of the parent	X	X
Non-controlling interest	X	X
	X	X

Foreign currency

Transactions undertaken in a foreign currency should be translated at the **rate in force at the transaction date**.

Where the exchange rate has changed by the settlement date, an exchange difference will be recognised in profit or loss.

Where the settlement date is in a subsequent accounting period, the amount outstanding should be restated at the year end at the **closing rate**. Any resulting exchange difference is recognised in profit or loss for the year.

Non-monetary items are not restated, they continue to be carried at the amount recognised at the transaction date.

(IAS 21: para. 21)

18: Earnings per share

Topic List

Basic EPS

Changes in capital structure

Diluted EPS

Earnings per share is a widely used measure of an entity's performance. It is useful for comparing the results of one entity over time and comparing the performance of an entity's equity against the performance of another entity's equity.

IAS 33 *Earnings per Share*

This standard aims to improve the **comparison** of different entities in the same period and of the same entity in different periods.

Basic calculation

$$\frac{\text{Net profit/loss attributable to ordinary shareholders}}{\text{Weighted average no. of shares in issue during the period}}$$

The net profit or loss used is after interest, tax and deductions in respect of non-equity shares.

(IAS 33: para. 10)

Changes in capital structure

It is necessary to match the earnings for the year against the capital base giving rise to those earnings.

Bonus issue

The earnings of the entity will not rise (no new funds injected); to calculate the number of shares:

Treat bonus shares as if in issue for the full year

Apply retrospectively, reducing the reported EPS for the previous year by the reciprocal of the bonus fraction

Issue at full market price

New capital is introduced therefore earnings would be expected to rise from date of new issue; to calculate the number of shares:

Use time weighted average number of shares for period

No retrospective effect

Rights issue

For purposes of calculating the number of shares, treat this as an issue at full market price followed by a bonus issue:

Use weighted average number of shares in issue for the period modified by the retrospective effect of the bonus element

Bonus element

$$\frac{\text{Actual cum} - \text{rights price}}{\text{Theoretical ex} - \text{rights price}}$$

(IAS 33: para. 26)

18: Earnings per share

Diluted EPS

Required where a listed entity has outstanding convertible loan notes, preferred shares, debentures, options or warrants

Must be shown on the face of the statement of profit or loss and other comprehensive income and given equal prominence with basic EPS

- Numerators of calculations must be disclosed. Denominators must be disclosed and reconciled to each other.

- Other amounts per share may be shown but profit used must be reconciled to a line item in the statement of profit or loss.

Convertible loan notes or preference shares

Earnings

Net basis earnings	X
Add back loan note interest net of tax (or preference dividends) 'saved'	X
Diluted earnings	X

No of shares

Basic weighted average	X
Add additional shares on conversion (use terms giving max dilution available after y/e)	X
Diluted number	X

(IAS 33: paras. 30–41)

19: Calculation and interpretation of accounting ratios and trends

Topic List

Profitability

Liquidity

Gearing

Investors' ratios

*The emphasis here is on **interpretation.** Calculation of ratios will provide only a fraction of available marks. There are many standard ratios, so variations of those shown here may come up and will be acceptable.*

The exercise must be done with a clear objective in mind – and apply your general financial knowledge, don't just rely on the ratios. And acceptable values will depend on industry, market strategy etc.

Return on capital employed

$$ROCE = \frac{PBIT}{Capital\ employed} = \frac{PBIT}{Total\ assets\ less\ current\ liabilities}$$

- When interpreting look for:
  - How risky is the business?
  - How capital intensive is it?
  - What ROCE do similar businesses have?
- Problems: which items to consider to achieve comparability?
  - Revaluation reserves
  - Policies, eg goodwill, R&D
  - Bank overdraft: short-long-term liability
  - Investments and related income: exclude
- Examine
  - Change year to year
  - Comparison to similar entities
  - Comparison with current market borrowing rates

Return on equity

$$ROE = \frac{PAT\ and\ pref\ div}{Ord\ share\ capital+reserves}\ \%$$

- More restricted view of capital than ROCE, but same principles

Profit margin

$$Profit\ margin = \frac{PBIT}{Sales}\%\quad Gross\ profit\ margin = \frac{Gross\ profit}{Sales}$$

- Useful to compare profit margin to profit % to investigate movements which do not match

Asset turnover

$$Asset\ turnover = \frac{Sales}{Total\ assets\ less\ current\ liabilities}$$

- Measures efficiency of use of assets; can amend to just non-current assets for capital intensive business

Current ratio

$$\text{Current ratio} = \frac{\text{Current assets}}{\text{Current liabilities}}$$

- Assume assets realised at book value
- 2:1 acceptable? 1.5:1? Depends on industry

Quick ratio

$$\text{Quick ratio (acid test)} = \frac{\text{Current assets} - \text{Inventory}}{\text{Current liabilities}}$$

- Eliminates illiquid and subjectively valued inventory
- Could be high if overtrading with rec'bles, but no cash
- 1:1 OK? But supermarkets etc on 0.3 (no rec'bles)

A/cs receivable collection period

$$\frac{\text{Trade receivables}}{\text{Credit sales}} \times 365$$

- Consistent with quick/current ratio? If not, investigate

Inventory turnover/days

$$\text{Turnover} = \frac{\text{Cost of sales}}{\text{Av inv}} \qquad \text{Days} = \frac{\text{Av inv}}{\text{Cost of sales}} \times 365$$

- Higher the better? But remember:
  - Lead times
  - Seasonal fluctuations in orders
  - Alternative uses of warehouse space
  - Bulk buying discounts
  - Likelihood of inventory perishing or becoming obsolete

A/cs payable payment period

$$\frac{\text{Trade accounts payable}}{\text{Purchases}} \times 365$$

- Use cost of sales if purchases not disclosed

Cash cycle

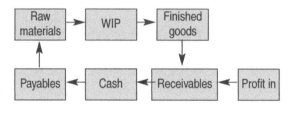

- Cash flow timing $\neq$ sales/cost of sales timing as credit is taken
- Holding inventory delays time between payments for goods to suppliers and sales receipts from customers

Why liquidity changes

- *Credit control efficiency* altered
- Altering *payment period of suppliers:* many companies in the recession used their suppliers as a source of funding
- *Inventory control:* in the recession many companies reduced their inventory holdings to maintain their liquidity

In an economic downturn, liquidity becomes a crucial issue.

Example
Just think of all those dot.com businesses!

Gearing

Gearing ratio = $\dfrac{\text{Prior charge capital}}{\text{Total capital}}$ %

Interest cover

Interest cover = $\dfrac{\text{PBIT (incl int receivable)}}{\text{Interest payable}}$

- Is interest cover a better way to measure gearing?
  - Company must generate enough profit to cover interest
  - Is 3+ safe? Consider relevance of profit vs cash

Debt/equity ratio

Debt/equity ratio = $\dfrac{\text{Prior charge capital}}{\text{Ordinary share capital and reserves}}$ %

(> 100% = high)

These ratios deal with long-term liquidity.

There are difficulties in assessing gearing:

- Use of equity accounting to lower gearing
- Elements included are subjective. Following could have an impact:
  - Convertible loan notes
  - Preference shares
  - Deferred tax
  - Goodwill and development expenditure capitalisation
  - Revaluation surplus

19: Calculation and interpretation of accounting ratios and trends

Used by someone contemplating investment. Consider an entity's shares as a source of income (dividends) and/or source of capital growth (share price).

Dividend yield

$$\text{Dividend yield} = \frac{\text{Div per share}}{\text{Mid-market price}} \%$$

- Low yield: retains large proportion of profits to reinvest
- High yield: risky company or slow-growing

Dividend cover

$$\text{Dividend cover} = \frac{\text{EPS}}{\text{Net div per ordinary share}} \quad \text{or}$$

$$\frac{\text{Profit after tax and pref div}}{\text{Div on ordinary shares}}$$

- Shows how safe the dividend is, or extent of profit retention. Variations due to maintaining dividend vs declining profits.

P/E ratio

$$\text{P/E ratio} = \frac{\text{Mid-market price}}{\text{EPS}}$$

- Higher the better; reflects confidence of market
- Rise in EPS will cause decrease in P/E ratio, but maybe not to same extent: context of market, industry norms

Earnings yield

$$\text{Earnings yield} = \frac{\text{EPS}}{\text{Mid-market price}}$$

- Shows dividend yield if no retention
- Compare entities with different dividend policies
- Shows growth rather than earnings

20: Limitations of financial statements and interpretation techniques

Topic List

Limitations of financial statements

Accounting policies and the limitations of ratio analysis

In this chapter we look at some of the issues which may make financial statements, and ratios based upon them, less reliable than they appear.

Limitations of financial statements

A number of factors may make financial statements less reliable than they appear:

- Problems of historic cost information – especially in periods of inflation
- Creative accounting – often aimed at reducing gearing
- The effect of related parties, in particular involving group companies
- Seasonal trading – timing of year end
- Asset acquisition – especially just before the year end

Accounting policies

Choice of accounting policy can affect the financial statements – such as whether to revalue assets or capitalise interest costs.

Change of accounting policy can only be justified on grounds of fairer presentation.

Limitations of ratio analysis

- In first year of trading no comparative figures
- Comparison against industry averages may not be very revealing
- If based on historic cost, undervalued assets may distort ROCE and gearing
- Ratios influenced by choice of accounting policy
- May be distorted by creative accounting measures
- Results may be distorted by inflation
- No two companies have the same risk profile, therefore comparison difficult

21: Statements of cash flows

Topic List

IAS 7 *Statement of Cash Flows*

Workings

Interpretation

Statements of cash flows were brought in because profit does not always give a useful picture of an entity's operations.

You've covered statements of cash flow earlier, so this should serve as revision.

Indirect method
STATEMENT OF CASH FLOWS FOR YEAR ENDED 31.12.X1
Cash flows from operating activities

Net profit before taxation	X
Adjustments for	
Depreciation	X
Investment income	(X)
Interest expense	X
Operating profit before working capital changes	X
Increase in trade and other receivables	(X)
Decrease in inventories	X
Decrease in trade payables	(X)
Cash generated from operations	X
Interest paid	(X)
Income taxes paid	(X)
Net cash from operating activities	X

Think carefully about what you are adding and subtracting.

(IAS 7: III Ex A)

Net cash from operating activities brought forward		X
Cash flows from investing activities		
Purchase of property, plant and equipment	(X)	
Proceeds from sale of equipment	X	
Interest received	X	
Dividends received	X	
		(X)
Cash flows from financing activities		
Proceeds from issuance of share capital	X	
Proceeds from long-term borrowings	X	
Payment of lease liabilities	(X)	
Dividends paid	(X)	
Net cash used in financing activities		(X)
Net increase in cash and cash equivalents		X
Cash and cash equivalents at beginning of period		X
Cash and cash equivalents at end of period		X

(IAS 7: III Ex A)

Cash equivalents

Short-term, highly liquid investments that are readily convertible to known amounts of cash and which are subject to an insignificant risk of changes in value

Note. *Cash and cash equivalents*

Cash and cash equivalents consist of cash on hand and balances with banks, and investments in money market instruments. Cash and cash equivalents included in the statement of cash flows comprise the following amounts.

	20X1	20X0
	$m	$m
Cash on hand and balances with banks	X	X
Short-term investments	X	X
Cash and cash equivalents	X	X

Direct method

The operating activities element of the cash flow statement is different.

	$'000
Cash flows from operating activities	
Cash receipts from customers	X
Cash paid to suppliers and employees	(X)
Cash generated from operations	X
Interest paid	(X)
Income taxes paid	(X)
Net cash from operating activities	X

(IAS 7: para. 7)

TAX PAID

Note. These can be presented as T accounts (shown here) or as shown in the corresponding text chapter.

		Deferred tax b/d	X
∴ Tax paid	X	Income tax b/d	X
		Charge for year	X
Deferred tax c/d	X		
Income tax c/d	X		
	$\overline{\underline{X}}$		$\overline{\underline{X}}$

LEASE LIABILITY

∴ Lease		B/d liability	
payments	X	< 1 year	X
		> 1 year	X
C/d liability		New lease in	
< 1 year	X	year	X
> 1 year	X		
	$\overline{\underline{X}}$		$\overline{\underline{X}}$

NON-CURRENT ASSETS

Bal b/d			
(NBV)	X	Depreciation	X
Revaluation	X		
∴ Addition	X		
		Bal c/d	
		(NBV)	X
	$\overline{\underline{X}}$		$\overline{\underline{X}}$

Extra information

Extra information not found in other primary statements:

- Relationships between profit and cash shown

- Cash equivalents are included in cash balances, giving a better picture of the liquidity of the company

- Financing inflows and outflows must be shown, rather than simply passed through reserves

Examining relationships

- Cash flow gearing: Compare operating cash flows and financing flows, particularly borrowing

- Operating cash flows to investment flows: Match cash recovery from investment to investment

- Investment to distribution: Indicates the proportion of total cash outflow designated specifically to investor return and reinvestment

22: Accounting for inflation

Topic List

Capital maintenance

CPP/CCA

There are different theories of capital maintenance.

In the UK, when inflation was high, attempts were made to introduce a form of CCA, but companies consistently ignored it and the standard was eventually abandoned.

Without the impetus of high inflation, there is unlikely to be any more need to address capital maintenance issues.

You are unlikely to be asked anything complex in these areas; make sure you can explain the main terms.

Financial capital maintenance

Under historical cost accounting (HCA), the amount maintained is the capital sum put into the business by the owner.

Focusing on the equity ownership of the entity is often referred to as the *proprietary concept of capital*: if we pay all profits out as dividends and inflation exists then in future our business will gradually run down, as our cash will become insufficient to buy replacement inventory.

Operating capital maintenance

Capital is looked at as the capacity to maintain a level of assets, alternatively referred to as the *physical capacity capital maintenance concept*, or the *entity concept*. By using replacement cost for our cost of sales we will set aside enough cash to buy replacement assets.

(IASB, *Conceptual Framework*: 4.59–4.65)

Current purchasing power (CPP)

The idea behind CPP accounting is that all accounts items are restated in terms of a stable monetary unit: The $CPP.

- Changes in purchasing power are based on the general level of inflation using the RPI

- CPP measures profits as the increase in the *current purchasing power* of equity; profits are stated after allowing for the declining purchasing power of money due to price inflation

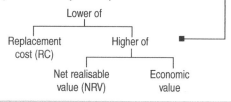

Lower of

Replacement cost (RC) — Higher of

Net realisable value (NRV) — Economic value

Current cost accounting (CCA)

CCA uses the operating capital maintenance concept. The assets consumed or sold, and those in the SFP, are stated at their value to the business, the deprival value, defined as shown in the diagram adjacent.

- Depreciation is charged on non-current assets on the basis of gross replacement cost of the asset (where RC is the deprival value)

- Where NRV or EV is the deprival value, the charge against CCA profits will be the loss in value of the asset during the accounting period

- Goods sold are charged at their replacement cost

- A typical set of CCA is prepared by adjusting SFP values with a supporting current cost reserve, and taking a HC P&L and making CCA adjustments

23: Specialised, not-for-profit and public sector entities

Topic List

Primary aims

Regulatory framework

Performance measurement

Any questions on this will only be general ones.

Primary aims

Public sector entities

Examples:

- Government departments
- Health services (if government funded)
- Education services

Aims:

- To provide services to the public
- To make good use of taxpayers' funds

Private sector entities

Examples:

- Charities

Aims:

- To provide services to beneficiaries
- To raise funds for this purpose

Regulatory framework

Public sector

International Public Sector Accounting Standards (IPSASs), based on IFRS

Private sector

Regulated nationally eg by Charities Commission in UK

Statement of Recommended Practice (SORP) 2005. Charities must use **accruals** basis (unless revenue below £100,000 p.a.) and apply UK standards.

In other countries, requirements will be different.

Performance measurement

Not judged by bottom line profit but must show that they have managed their funds properly.

Performance measured in terms of **achievement of stated purpose**.

Possible performance measures are:

- **3Es** – Economy, Efficiency, Effectiveness
- **KPIs** – Key performance indicators – specific to that organisation
- **VFM** – Value for money – and **best value** for outside services
- **Impact report** – produced by some charities to show measure of achievement – what impact did they have?